MW00947070

Emotional Intelligence

The Essential Guide to Improving Your Social Skills, Relationships and Boosting Your EQ

© **Copyright 2018 by –David Clark- All rights reserved.**

This document is geared towards providing exact and reliable information regarding topic and issue covered. The publication is sold with the idea that the publisher is not required to render accounting, officially permitted, or otherwise, qualified services. If advice is necessary, legal or professional, a practiced individual in the profession should be ordered.

- From a Declaration of Principles which was accepted and approved equally by a Committee of the American Bar Association and a Committee of Publishers and Associations.

In no way is it legal to reproduce, duplicate, or transmit any part of this document in either electronic means or in printed format. Recording of this publication is strictly prohibited and any storage of this document is not allowed unless with written permission from the publisher. All rights reserved.

The information provided herein is stated to be truthful and consistent, in that any liability, in terms of inattention or otherwise, by any usage or abuse of any policies, processes, or directions contained within is the solitary and utter responsibility of the recipient reader. Under no circumstances will any legal responsibility or blame be held against the publisher for any reparation, damages, or monetary loss due to the information herein, either directly or indirectly.

Respective authors own all copyrights not held by the publisher.

The information herein is offered for informational purposes solely, and is universal as so. The presentation of the information is without contract or any type of guarantee assurance.

The trademarks that are used are without any consent, and the publication of the trademark is without permission or backing by the trademark owner. All trademarks and brands within this book are for clarifying purposes only and are the owned by the owners themselves, not affiliated with this document.

Table of Contents

Introduction

Emotional Intelligence has grown to be a popular phrase over the past decade. Everyone is talking about how important it is when it comes to enjoying professional success and fulfilling interpersonal relationships. Yet, surprisingly, not many people seem to know what emotional intelligence, also known as emotional quotient, actually is or how to improve it.

Countless studies have made shocking revelations about how emotional quotient (EQ) is far more important than intelligence quotient (IQ) when it comes to not just success at work but also social and personal relationships. The good news is, unlike intelligence quotient (which is largely determined by genetics), emotional quotient can be constantly enhanced.

Yes, we can continue to increase our emotional intelligence through consistent practice. Research undertaken in multiple universities across North America and Europe have indicated that while intelligence quotient accounts for only 20 percent of our success and accomplishments, emotional intelligence plays a staggering 80 percent role in it.

This simply means that if you are not able to deal with, identify and manage your emotions and the emotions of other people, you are less likely to succeed in many aspects of life. All technical skills, experience, qualification and even intelligence are important, however, people who have the ability to deal with their own emotions and other people's emotions are the type of people who quickly rise to leadership roles.

Two psychologists, John Mayer and Peter Salovey, coined the term 'emotional quotient' in 1990 as a social alternative for intelligence quotient, which fundamentally dealt with a person's cognitive abilities. News spread wildly around the globe that human beings had two types of brains or intelligence—the original one that is related to rational, logical and cognitive functions, and the newly discovered one that is related to processing feelings and emotions. Suddenly, emotional intelligence was the buzzword that got everyone's attention, including large corporations around the world. It became one of the most crucial parameters for employee or workforce selection for hiring managers.

In a startling study, top leaders of 200 of the nation's biggest companies were carefully studied.

It emerged that they did have some characteristics in common. Corporate leaders were exceptionally good at academic knowledge, technical skills, and the ability to manage their own emotions. Surprisingly, emotional intelligence contributed twice as much to their success than all other three factors put together. This clearly shows that intelligence alone doesn't take us too far in life unless it is backed by the ability to understand and manage our (and other people's) emotions.

While intelligence and technical ability can ascertain if you will be a good fit for a particular industry or role, it is your ability to manage emotions that will determine how good you are at performing the role.

Another study conducted on students by Yale University Center for emotional intelligence concluded that adolescents who possess high emotional intelligence are less anxious, are seldom bogged down by depression and are less likely to resort to addictions (alcohol, drugs, cigarettes etc.). They are also less aggressive and less likely to display signs of becoming a bully. Their attention span is higher; they tend to be less hyper and are known to display leadership skills. These students also excel at academics and the ability to cope with challenges related to it. It is remarkable how much of an impact emotional intelligence can have on social skills, academic performance and gaining knowledge.

Does this mean that we should focus only on emotional intelligence and not on cognitive or rational intelligence? No, not at all because both are important. However, intellectual prowess without the ability to manage emotions won't lead us on a path to success because at the end of the day we have to deal with people all the time.

Similarly, emotional intelligence without technical skills and IQ will not lead us in the right direction. If anything, emotional quotient and intelligence quotient both complement each other to ensure overall success in different spheres of an individual's life.

Contrary to what people mistakenly believe, emotional quotient is not the rival of intelligence quotient. It is an ally. Our life is a huge social construct with complex and intricately woven social dynamics. How far do you think your cognitive ability can take you? Theodore Roosevelt hit the nail on the head when he famously uttered the words, "No one cares how much you know until they know how much you care." These words capture the essence of emotional intelligence and the very core of being a human who operates well in a social environment.

Emotional quotient spans several areas of our mental well-being, social relationships, interpersonal equations with people and much more. People who are emotionally intelligent demonstrate better mental health and well-being; they are also better equipped to lead and inspire people and enjoy more rewarding personal relationships. Therefore, the ability to manage relationships more efficiently and resolve conflicts can lead to overall greater success in life.

The benefits of possessing a high emotional quotient aren't limited to our personal life alone. EQ is applicable to our professional life as well. It is often noticed that people with average intelligence often surpass those with very high intelligence to achieve unimaginable professional success. We often wonder how X has been quickly promoted into a leadership role over Y when Y is more technically knowledgeable and intelligent. The answer most probably lies in X's ability to deal with his or her and others' emotions.

According to a study conducted by the Center for Creative Leadership, 75 percent of all careers go astray owing to emotional incompetency, the inability to deal with interpersonal issues, unsatisfactory leadership skills during crisis or conflicts, the inability to inspire people's trust and failure to adapt.

The great news is that your emotional quotient is not etched in stone. It isn't something that can never be altered. It takes lots of work but increasing it is pretty attainable if you are willing to put in the necessary work. Emotional intelligence can hugely impact all aspects of your life to help you enjoy greater happiness, gain contentment and improve your well-being. Throughout this book, we'll talk about solid, powerful strategies that you can start using right away for increasing your emotional quotient and social skills. It will help give you more purpose and build more productive interpersonal relationships.

Chapter One: Dangers of Reduced Social Intelligence

Social intelligence is characterized by the ability to build successful social relationships and overcome challenging social environments. It is our ability to connect with and deal with other people in a social set-up scenario. As a society, we are obsessed with intelligence and academic smartness. However, our relationships play a much bigger role in our overall development and well-being. Of course, you need to be academically sound to enjoy professional success but you also need to be socially smart to lead people and build strong relationships.

However, have you wondered what happens when you are not socially adept or intelligent?

Lack of Empathy

Imagine a scenario where a person who is not socially intelligent comes to you and tries to offer condolences on the death of a family member. You get his or her phone call to offer condolence. They talk about how sorry they are for your loss but you get a feeling they don't really mean it and are doing it more out of a sense of obligation. You can hear them speaking to someone else in the background and typing on a keyboard—basically, they are preoccupied with something else and are only offering their regret about your loss as an obligation without actually empathizing with you. How do you end up feeling after the rather insincere, ice cold and mechanical condolence? It makes you feel even worse than you felt before they called.

Socially unintelligent folks lack the ability to empathize with other people and their troubles, which makes it challenging for them to form strong and mutually fulfilling bonds with others.

Not Being Flexible or Agreeable

Be honest and answer this. Do you like people who always take the high road around you? Nope, no one does really! These are people who are extremely rigid about their views, are not open to suggestions, don't believe in working out a way to meet in the middle, and don't appreciate even constructive criticism from others. It is either my way or the highway for them. If you are one of these people, you are sooner or later going to struggle with social relationships. A huge component of emotional and social intelligence is being open, agreeable and flexible.

If you are a rigid and closed person, people may pretend to be nice to you on the outside but deep on the inside, they don't really appreciate your tendency to dictate terms all the time. Before you know it, they'll start avoiding you and minimizing interaction with you. Social intelligence is about accepting and respecting other people's perspectives even if it is different from your own. It is about being flexible enough to identify and incorporate the good in other people's suggestions. It helps you gain a different perspective and puts you on the same page as the other person to connect in a more harmonious manner. People will appreciate having you around them and listening to your perspective in an open and agreeable manner.

Social Anxiety and Social Triggers

People who lack social intelligence often become increasingly anxious in a social situation, which hinders their ability to connect with people.

What are the triggers that are causing this social anxiety? As a child, you may not have had many people attending your birthday party. This has been firmly embedded in your mind even though you've grown up now, and things have changed a lot. Today, you may have plenty of people who would willingly attend your party but disappointing and negative thoughts about your childhood birthday party prevent you from inviting your friends to celebrate with you.

Identifying your social triggers can help combat social anxiety.

- What are the types of social situations that make you anxious?

- What type of interactions make you want to quickly escape from the place?

- When do you get a feeling that you can't really be yourself?

Socially anxious people find it challenging to conduct themselves in social scenarios, to fulfill social relationships and professionally network with people from within their industry. They are basically operating in isolation which doesn't help them leverage the power of social contacts and belonging in a community.

Lack of Understanding of Other People's Emotions

A person I knew (let's call her Anne for this example) was exceptionally good where technical knowledge, ability and potential were concerned. Anne was able to get things done and drive commendable results. However, her approach to getting those results wasn't very favorable and didn't find many takers, which made her an unpopular manager. Anne was known to demean others, display impatience and sport a rather dogmatic attitude. She left a lot of people disappointed and unmotivated, which didn't go down well in her feedback. When confronted about the feedback others gave against her, Anne was shocked. She didn't see it this way and was surprised others found her dictatorial.

For Anne, she was only getting people to perform according to the demands of the projects. This lack of self-awareness and lack of understanding about how she impacted other people's emotions led to Anne's downfall. Imagine an otherwise ace professional struggling with lack of self-awareness and a sense of empathy.

What Anne was saying was, "At the end of it all, it is about results and getting stuff done." What her team and subordinates were interpreting was, "I don't care about anything but results, and in the process, if I hurt your feelings, it doesn't matter." There was a clear gap between what Anne thought she was coming across as and what she was actually coming across as. This disconnect is what caused her professional downfall!

Socially and emotionally intelligent people can identify not just their own feelings but also the impact they have on other people's emotions. They can recognize and perceive other people's emotions and manage them in the best interests of everyone involved. Unlike Anne, they know the impact their actions or emotions have on others and therefore, alter their own emotional behavior to positively influence other people's actions.

You may have all the intelligence, academic excellence and experience in the world, but if you don't know how to deal with your emotions and other people's emotions, you aren't going to get far in your professional and personal life.

Signs that you lack social and emotional intelligence:

- You often think people are being too sensitive to your humor or jokes and are overreacting.

- You jump into any conversation with absolute assertiveness and refuse to budge most of the time.

You are also quick to defend your stand with gusto should anyone even question it reasonably.

- You think social popularity and being liked in your workplace is grossly overrated. As long as you do your work and deliver results, it shouldn't matter whether people like you or not.

- You have extremely high expectations of yourself and others, many times bordering on unreasonable and impractical.

- You get irritated and frustrated when others expect you to understand how they feel. Your thought process is, "How am I supposed to know or understand someone else's feelings without them talking to me about it?"

- Most of the time you feel like people don't understand your point or know where you are coming from, which makes you annoyed and upset.

- You always find yourself blaming other people and circumstances for your shortcomings and failures.

You seldom accept responsibility and accountability for your acts, and you pass the buck elsewhere.

Of course, it isn't just limited to these signs. There are many other indicators of low social and emotional intelligence, though these are typical signs that most people with low emotional and social intelligence display.

Chapter Two: Components of Emotional Intelligence

I bet you all know at least one person (or it could be you are that person) who is always calm and composed even while handling the most socially awkward and volatile situation. They handle disagreements with grace, play mediators with ease and are top notch at negotiating difficult deals. These are the people who always make everyone feel comfortable and heard.

Emotional intelligence is all about a person's ability to identify and manage emotions, which is relevant in all spheres of life from academics to personal relationships to professional development. Whether you are a decision maker or homemaker, you'll need emotional intelligence to survive in a social setup that is fraught with complex relationship dynamics.

So, what exactly is emotional intelligence comprised of?

Psychologist and bestselling author of the book entitled *Emotional Intelligence*, Daniel Goleman, suggested five basic components that make up emotional intelligence. Look at each of them and identify areas that you can improve on for increasing your emotional intelligence.

Self-Awareness

Self-awareness is the ability to identify or understand one's own emotions. Actually, it goes beyond simply understanding your emotions. Self-awareness is also being able to manage your emotions and understand their impact on other people. It is about knowing how your mood, behavior, attitude and feelings can affect others around you and therefore, managing your emotions to create the desired effect on others.

You can only manage or control your behavior if you recognize your emotions and emotional responses. When you know that a certain emotion leads to a specific emotional reaction, you'll be able to manage that reaction more effectively. Self-awareness gives you a greater insight into your strengths and weaknesses. You make yourself open to fresh information and experiences and learn from your interaction with people.

According to Goleman, self-aware folks have a wonderful sense of humor, can view the positives in any situation, are self-assured about their abilities and are fully aware of the impact they have on others or how others see them.

Apart from being able to identify your emotions and being able to understand their impact on other people, emotionally intelligent people can regulate, control and manage their emotions, too. They seldom react on impulse or give in to involuntary responses. Their responses are more well-thought and considered. This doesn't imply that emotionally intelligent people hide their true emotions or don't express their emotions freely. It only means they are smart enough to understand the right place and time to express those emotions in an appropriate manner.

People who are high in self-regulation are more flexible, agreeable and have the ability to adapt effectively to change. They are wonderful at conflict management and diffusing potentially volatile situations. The increased self-regulation also leads to a greater sense of conscientiousness. These folks have a good grip on the impact they have on others and accept responsibility for their behavior.

Motivation

Motivation plays a critical role in emotional intelligence because emotionally intelligent people are intrinsically motivated by elements that go beyond recognition, rewards, money, fame and other similar things. Instead, they are driven by an inner desire to fulfill their objectives and passions. They crave internal rewards and gain their high from doing things they love.

People who are intrinsically motivated are more action-oriented when it comes to setting and fulfilling goals. They have a high need for accomplishment and are constantly looking for ways to improve their performance. Emotionally intelligent people are more committed to taking initiatives and looking for better ways to accomplish even higher results. They will aim to fulfill any task to the best of their abilities.

Empathy

Empathy is the ability to put yourself in another person's shoes to understand things from his or her perspective. This one component is often believed to be the cornerstone of emotional intelligence. Empathy goes beyond trying to identify how the other person is feeling. It is about recognizing and understanding the other person's emotional state as well as knowing how best to respond to the person's emotions based on the available emotional information.

For example, if you get the feeling that the other person is feeling depressed or dejected, you may interact with them in a more thoughtful, considerate and sensitive manner. You may make an additional effort to cheer up their spirits and make them feel good. Basically, you've used information about their emotions to behave in a manner that influences them in a positive way.

Being empathetic allows you to be a good leader and understand the feelings of your team or followers without much effort. This is especially true in professional settings, where leaders are required to inspire and influence the workforce into fulfilling the organization's goals. Empathetic leaders understand power dynamics and social relationships, along with how their behavior can impact these forces in various situations.

Sometimes, employees may perform well, but there may still be a sense of frustration, stress and dissatisfaction owing to long work hours or meeting crucial deadlines. As a leader, your technical skills will only help you impart knowledge to the team. However, keeping both their spirits and morale high is something you can accomplish only with both empathy and emotional intelligence.

In such a scenario, you have to be a perceptive leader to determine the feelings of your team and use this information to direct your behavior and actions towards lifting their morale.

Empathy is perceptiveness of the other person's emotions and feelings, and taking a keen interest in issues they are grappling with. It is also the ability to predict the other person's requirements and take the appropriate action.

Social Skills

Much of our emotional skills have to do with being able to interact and connect with others to form mutually fulfilling or rewarding social or interpersonal relationships. Identifying and managing your feelings and the feelings of other people are only half the battle won. You need to actually put this information to use in your everyday interaction, association and communication with others.

In your personal life, developing social skills may make you the ultimate girl or guy magnet. Similarly, within the professional set up, you may need to build a strong rapport with your manager and colleagues. Some of the most important social skills involve active listening, nonverbal communication (expressions, gestures, posture, etc.), persuasiveness, verbal communication (tone of voice) and leadership skills.

Social skills involve communicating effectively, practicing active listening and responding to the person appropriately. It is also about being able to guide, lead and inspire people. One of the most important aspects of social skills is conflict management, or the ability to diffuse challenging situations with negotiation, diplomacy and persuasion.

Social skills can also be termed as relationship management, where an inspiring guide or leader becomes a catalyst for change, leading people to achieve a higher level of performance and helping them adapt to change. In short, it is about the finesse with which one deals with other people.

Chapter Three: Identifying and Articulating Emotions

One of the most important components of emotional intelligence is the ability to identify and manage your own emotions and other people's emotions. When you learn to observe your emotions and express them in a manner that is beneficial for the overall situation, you display high emotional intelligence. The unfortunate truth is that not many are adept at recognizing and articulating their emotions.

Sometimes, all we need to do to display high emotional intelligence is observe our emotions or feelings in a non-judgmental manner. The good news is, a person can increase his or her emotional intelligence by displaying a high understanding of his or her emotions through consistent practice. Here are a few tips for identifying or recognizing your emotions and expressing them:

Observe Your Feelings throughout the Day

Practice observing and identifying your feelings all day. How do certain experiences at various points in time during the day make you feel? When people say something that angers you, carefully note what exactly they've said to trigger the feeling of anger. This will help you develop a wide range of emotional vocabulary. I would even go a step further and say, for the purpose of quickly and easily identifying them, give your emotions names.

Labeling emotions makes it easier to identify specific emotions because even emotions like anger can have several different forms. For instance, it can be anger out of humiliation or anger induced by a feeling of jealousy or anger owing to expectations that arc not met.

Naming your emotions makes it easier to identify and manage them. This practice also lets you take a step back from reacting impulsively and focusing on the cognitive parts of the brain for resolving issues. It will help you understand and make sense of your feelings more effectively. The practice gives you a better understanding of making choices when it comes to interacting with others.

You can note your reactions to events throughout the day in a journal as they occur. Avoid ignoring it because you're overlooking important information that can have a huge effect on your thinking and actions. Consciously pay more attention to your emotions and link them to everyday experiences.

For example, you are in a meeting, trying to make offers and suggestions, and a co-worker just cuts you off and takes the conversation elsewhere. What emotions do you feel at this point in time? Similarly, a few minutes later, your manager appreciates you for a task well done. What are the emotions and feelings you experience? When you get into the habit of clearly identifying emotions (and labeling them) such as anger, embarrassment, sorrow, elation, peace, contentment, envy, frustration, annoyance, etc., your emotional intelligence automatically increases. Start tapping into your emotions at specific points during the day. For instance, what is the first emotion you feel on waking up? What are the feelings you experience before falling asleep?

Practice Deep Breathing and Mindfulness

All our emotions are experienced physically. When we are angry, upset or stressed, the feelings manifest themselves through our body. Our bodies respond on an evolutionary level (instinctively or involuntarily) like they would respond to a natural threat. Some physiological reactions to our emotions can be a speeding heartbeat, increased pulse rate, sweating, shallow breathing and more.

When we calm down these physiological reactions, we quickly bring about a change in our feelings and emotions too. When you kill physical stress, the mental stress naturally melts away. Each time you find yourself feeling stressed or tensed, take a slow, deep breath. Focus completely on your breath and practice deep breathing. Pay attention to how it feels to have oxygen enter your lungs. Notice how your mouth, throat, lungs and abdomen feel when you breathe in and breathe out. Concentrate on the flow of air in and out of the abdominal cavity. Taking even a few deep breaths will make you feel better, and you will be in a positive frame of mind while interacting with other people.

Each time you find yourself diverting focus away from your breath, gently acknowledge the feeling without judging it and move the focus back to your breath. Stay in the present moment in a purposeful manner. Avoid thinking about the past or future and focus only on the breath. Your emotional frequency will change in no time.

Practice mindfulness (focusing attention on the present moment in a purposeful and non-judgmental manner) in all spheres of life to calm down your spirit (especially if you happen to be a more hot-tempered or easily irritable individual).

By practicing to observe your emotions and feelings in a non-judgmental manner, you not only boost your awareness of these feelings with greater clarity, but also reduce your chances of being overwhelmed by a bunch of negative or destructive emotions.

Question Your Perspective

The first step towards increasing your emotional intelligence and social skills is recognizing that there are multiple ways of looking at a situation. Even though you may completely believe that your perspective or way of looking at things is right, get into the habit of considering it from different angles rather than giving in to knee-jerk responses.

When you are angry or upset with someone, avoid reacting impulsively. Instead, slow down and consider various ways of explaining the circumstances. What are the different ways to explain the situation? Of course, you may still stick to your perspective but at least attempt to look at it from various angles before considering the situation in a calmer and more rational manner. At best, even if your perspective about the situation doesn't change, you'll get more time to calm down and think of a more positive, constructive response.

Celebrate Positive Emotions to Attract More of Them

Emotionally intelligent folks who experience greater positive energy lead more fulfilling relationships and are more resilient when it comes to responding to negative situations. Therefore, get into the habit of intentionally doing things that induce a sense of happiness and joy within you.

There are several ways to bring more joy into your spirit including performing random acts of kindness, practicing gratitude, being in the midst of nature, exercising, engaging in productive hobbies, creative visualization and reminiscing about past experiences that have brought you happiness. Celebrating positive emotions helps you attract more of this positive mindset, and it helps create positive experiences.

Know Yourself like No One Else

The epicenter of emotional intelligence is knowing yourself like no one else. Self-awareness is the key to developing greater emotional intelligence. Having a good understanding of your core characteristics, strengths, weaknesses, beliefs, values, attitude and other similar aspects of your personality helps you understand your positive and negative triggers.

You will understand what drives your responses and how you can manage them more effectively if you gain complete self-awareness. A person can gain higher self-awareness through personality tests, reflection, feedback from others and more.

Try to establish a link between your emotions and the actions or behavior resulting from those emotions. What drives your impulses? Which specific emotions spur you to behave the way you do?

Solicit Feedback and Constructive Criticism

One of the best ways to gain greater self-awareness is to obtain feedback from trusted friends and family members. Ask people whom you've known for a long time to give you honest, genuine and constructive feedback about your strengths and areas of development.

You may agree or disagree with them, but you'll get a good idea about the effect your emotions and actions have on others, thus shielding you from blind spots. You will recognize the effect your behavior has on others whether you intend to create that effect or not. Sometimes, even we are unaware of the effect we have on others.

For example, you may be an extremely bold, confident, opinionated and self-assured individual. For you, this is a positive personality and a sign of being totally in control. However, for others, you may come across as overbearing, dogmatic and having a high tendency to hijack every conversation. Soliciting honest feedback from others will help you recognize this gap between how you perceive yourself and how others see you. This can help you change your behavior slightly to adapt to other people's emotions and create the desired impact on them.

Avoid Judgmental Emotions

Every emotion you feel is valid, even the seemingly negative ones. When we are judgmental about our emotions, it inhibits our ability to fully experience these emotions. Thus we are unable to use our emotions in positive, constructive ways. Rather than seeing them as negative or positive, view your emotions as information pieces that are closely linked to things happening within and around you.

It may not be as easy as it sounds. However, practicing to let both negative and positive emotions surface and linking them to things happening around you will help you understand them better. For instance, you may feel pangs of jealousy for someone, which can give you a good idea of the circumstance or situation. Similarly, linking positive emotions with events occurring around you will help you understand the link between your emotions and those events, so you know how to experience more of these feelings and emotions.

Observe your emotional history patterns. When you experience a powerful emotion, ask yourself when was the last time you experienced this emotion. When was the last time you felt something similar, and how did you feel before and after the situation? You will be able to manage your behavior more effectively when you can identify a clear pattern. You get to decide what you want to do differently only if you know how you usually react to these kinds of situations.

Chapter Four: Releasing Destructive Emotions and Strengthening Positive Ones

Feelings and emotions are a huge part of an individual's personality and interaction with other humans. If you don't control or manage them, they control and manage you. Negative emotions, at times, overpower us and take complete control of our life. However, you can learn to deal with these negative emotions by diverting your attention and investing the energy into something more positive and constructive. Train your brain to move out of the negative thinking cycle and get into a more positive frame of mind. Here are a few proven tips to release destructive emotions:

Intense Physical Activity

Releasing negative emotions from the mind is facilitated when you perform a physically demanding task such as exercising, kickboxing, running, working out at the gym, swimming and other similar activities. When you get active and exercise, the body releases feel-good hormones and chemicals that help elevate your mood. The feel-good

Endorphins promote a positive state of mind and act as a channel for venting out negative emotions.

Exercise is great for the body, mind and spirit! Participate in activities that preoccupy your body and mind, which means you'll have little time to process negative emotions. Sometimes, walking outdoors for even 15 minutes can give you a huge emotional boost. The idea is to occupy your mind with something else by changing its focus or putting yourself in a different environment.

A majority of the time, when something negative or unfortunate happens, we experience a strong wave of emotions. Wait for this wave to subside and then calmly contemplate how you wish to behave. Instead of bottling up or repressing your feelings and emotions, you need to decide how you want to express them. Avoid taking the escapist route in such a scenario by consuming excessive alcohol, doing drugs or spending hours watching television.

Instead, get up and get an outlet for these feelings by practicing a rigorous physical activity or talking to a trusted friend or family member.

Put on Your Creative Hat

Another wonderful way to release negative emotion is to channel it through artistic pursuits or passions. You can use art or other forms of creativity for restructuring your negative feelings and emotions into something constructive and positive, thus taking the focus away from these destructive feelings.

The negative emotions that occupy your mind disappear temporarily and give you time to contemplate or think through your actions. You get enough time to reflect upon your feelings and respond to them in a rational manner that's well thought out. Creativity can be anything from making a sculpture to developing a short story to going out and painting a happy scene on canvas. Divert your feelings towards writing a poem or song. If nothing else works, just turn on the music and dance. I swear, it works like magic.

Art and creativity allow you to transform destructive feelings into a more positive and constructive purpose, which helps curb anxiety, depression, frustration and stress. You will identify a clear purpose even in the pain.

If you are not the artistic type, even a regular adult coloring book and some crayons can do the trick. It's not a high skill activity and can be extremely cathartic all the same. Art and creativity have plenty of stress beating benefits.

Practice a 'Let Go' Ritual

It is extremely therapeutic to sometimes give in and vent your negative feelings or emotions (towards yourself or others) through a specific symbolic ritual. This is a tangible way, or physical way, to release negative emotional experiences. There are several rituals for releasing negative emotions.

I know some people who write a letter to themselves or another person expressing their thoughts, hurt, frustration, anger and anguish. Once they are done pouring their heart out into the paper, they burn or tear the letter, thus signifying that they are over their emotions or they have released those toxic emotions.

Throw the ashes in the air or flush them in the toilet. It is cleansing your body and mind from all negative emotions or flushing out destructive emotions. Mention all the emotions you've experienced and all steps you've wanted to take.

Spend Time with Loved Ones

One of the best ways to get negative emotions out of your mind is to spend time with loved ones who motivate and inspire you. Understanding, encouraging and supportive family members and friends can quickly change your mood and help you deal with painful emotions.

Though negative emotions are a part of life and allow us to grow stronger, we don't have to deal with it all alone. We can reach out to others and seek their support. This is also a great way to build a comforting circle that you can trust and turn to in challenging times. You can seek comfort, guidance and positivity from people who care about your well-being. So, the next time you are feeling dejected and down, simply talk to a trusted friend or family member and pour your heart out and watch as the frequency of your thoughts magically transform.

Talking to another person may help you gain a different perspective on your situation. You may begin to see things in a manner you hadn't considered earlier. Sometimes it is important to get a different and fresher perspective on your issues to resolve them. Look at others for guidance, advice, consolation and feedback. It isn't necessary to pretend to be strong all the time and handle everything on your own.

Reaching out to others is not a sign of weakness. Rather, it shows you are strong enough to ask for help to reduce your pain.

Avoid Dwelling on Problems

However badly you may feel about your problems or are upset about something, avoid dwelling on the issue. Ruminating about the problems only worsens it. Just try to understand it in a more objective manner. Don't make mountains out of molehills by focusing on negative emotions. I have a few tips up my sleeve when it comes to avoiding rumination and obsessing about issues.

One thing I love to do when I find myself being tempted to ruminate about an issue is, schedule a worry period for a few minutes each. I know it sounds incredulous to some. How can you set aside a worry period? It isn't some kind of rehearsal, is it? However, it can work miraculously well! Try to think about the issue for no longer than 25-30 minutes each day. As time passes, the feelings will gradually become fainter and less overpowering. Push the feelings away if they persist and remind yourself to wait until tomorrow's worry period.

Try to recognize the triggers that lead to rumination. For instance, why did you feel badly about the feedback your boss offered? Why are you so consumed by it? Is it related to worry about your performance, and subsequently, money? Are you worried about the impression your boss has about you? Identify the worst that can happen in the given scenario and determine different ways to handle the issue. Having a plan of action ready for dealing with the worst will put you in a more confident state of mind about niggling issues.

Problem-Resolution Approach

Sometimes we feel something about an issue or person because of an underlying cause. For instance, you may feel pangs of jealousy every time a co-worker outperforms you or is praised by your manager. This may have an underlying issue such as being burdened by expectations since childhood or that you were never praised enough by your family on your accomplishments. These feelings from your childhood that left you with low self-esteem and a sense of inadequacy may lead you to feel jealous or envious of other people. The underlying causes are low self-esteem or low morale.

Once you identify the underlying cause, it is easier to take remedial action against this overpowering feeling that is causing your negative emotions. You may decide to talk to a counselor or therapist to get rid of the underlying feeling of inadequacy and develop greater self-confidence, thus leading to the gradual elimination of feelings related to jealousy at work and personal relationships.

Let us look at another example. You may not be good at a particular technical skill, which makes you experience feelings of inadequacy or frustration. What can you do to eliminate the underlying issue that is causing the emotion? Get a tutor for the skill or ask a friend who is an expert to train you in it. You can also practice by taking on extra work, read or use online or offline study resources.

This is a remedial action for tackling the problem from its roots to discard the negative emotions it creates. Think of every possible solution and chalk out a plan for tackling the emotion from its roots rather than obsessing about it.

Challenge Negative Thoughts

Each time you find yourself slipping into a negative and irrational thought process, challenge the extreme or catastrophic thinking. Consider how you are responding to the situation. Try to avoid thinking in extremes and challenge unfounded thoughts. Why do you think XYZ doesn't care about you? What is the evidence that makes you think so? What is the evidence that challenges this thinking? Think about all the things that XYZ has done that shows they care.

Sometimes, we don't have solid evidence and tend to over think or exaggerate situations. Ask yourself questions such as, "Do I have evidence that my thoughts are true?" "Do I have evidence that these thoughts are untrue?" "Is there a different perspective on this issue?" "Am I intermingling facts with my opinion or beliefs?" "What can I do to deal with the situation in a more mature manner?" "How would someone I greatly admire or look up to react in a similar situation?"

Each time you find yourself being overcome by negative thoughts, replace it with more rational or realistic thoughts. Alter your self-talk from negative to neutral or positive. Keep repeating positive affirmations in your head like a tape. Make a conscious, mindful effort to think of a more realistic and optimistic way to look at the situation.

For instance, if a potential client who has taken your business card tells you that they'll call you for business in a low days and they don't, don't automatically assume that you've lost them or they won't call. Maybe they are pre-occupied with something important and will call you in few days. Maybe they have postponed the project for later and will call you when it is time to begin. Stay hopeful and relational. Don't automatically assume the worst until you have clear evidence of it.

When you change your self-talk, you alter your mood. Positive self-talk can completely transform the way you feel. Whenever you find the negative self-talk rambling in your head such as, "I am not good at something," or, "Someone is avoiding me," replace it with, "I am getting better at this each day," or, "They are preoccupied with something really important."

If you have been thinking negatively for long, you won't be able to switch to positive thoughts easily. In such a scenario, you'll find greater success with neutral or realistic thoughts.

Chapter Five: NLP and Thought Reframing

Submodalities are nothing but distractions that are made in our representational system. It assists in neurologically remembering sensory experiences both real and imagined. For example, there are higher chances of you remembering a vibrant, large image than a tiny dull-colored one. Submodalities are solid building blocks that feed our brain with what is important and what is not. Think of them as barcodes that help us identify specific sensory experiences and determine their importance.

If you understand coding, you'll know that even a slight change in the code can change the design or meaning. Changing or altering the meaning leads to a change in our state of mind. A change in the state of mind leads to changes in responses, which eventually reflects in our behavior. Doing things differently can help us change our reality as well as our perception of the world or reality.

What Is Reframing in NLP (Neuro-Linguistic Programming)?

In NLP, content reframe refers to offering a different meaning to a thought or statement by obtaining more content that completely changes or reframes the focus of your thought.

In reframing, you take an undesirable behavior or characteristic and lend it a more positive intention. You give more alternatives to fulfill the positive intent, trained by negotiations and rationalization for resolving mental conflict. Reframing thoughts can also change the entire meaning or context of the issue.

Even with NLP, reframing is all about changing the meaning or frequency of a thought either purposefully or unknowingly. Framing offers focus or border to your thought. You see a situation or issue within a specific reference, which is a direct result of your perceptions and beliefs. When you challenge these frames or limits, you change the way you perceive or react to a situation or experience.

For instance, your thoughts will drastically function differently when you are told that a task needs to be completed within an hour than when you are told that you have a fortnight to complete it. The objective of reframing is to assist a person in perceiving or experiencing the situation in a different way, which impacts your choices. Reframing your thoughts makes you more resourceful when it comes to reacting to a situation.

In NLP content reframing, a statement or situation is recovered using more information to change the entire context or focus (termed as reframing). Reframing simply means taking an undesirable action or trait and lending it a more positive intention.

Behavioral Techniques for Reframing Thoughts

Cognitive Behavior Therapy is utilized by professional therapists or counselors to help clients overcome negative or destructive thought patterns, and replace the same with more constructive and positive thoughts. Reframed thoughts can help enhance your outlook, which can lead to a more positive approach and action. Our negative thoughts or perceptions are often deeply rooted in childhood or adolescent experiences. CBT can form new neural pathways to change your thoughts and increase the horizons of your thought process. If anything, you are reprogramming your mind to influence your actions more positively.

Brainstorming

Brainstorming is a great way to identify your thoughts and then subsequently reframe them. Writing a journal can help your thoughts flow freely or unhindered. Attempt to identify your problem in a single sentence. Think of every possible solution that you can. Allow your imaginative problem-solving skills to freely come up with different possibilities.

For instance, if your lack of monetary resources is a burning issue, you can apply for a job, get a degree, consider applying for a loan or look at taking up another part-time job to supplement your current income. Getting back to the point, there are several possibilities when it comes to resolving an issue. You just have to consider these possibilities and award yourself some much-needed hope.

Use the Power of Visualization

Every time you rise each morning, and even before you move out of your bed, start visualizing your day. How do you want the day to unfold? What is the most positive outcome that you expect out of it? If you have a dentist's appointment scheduled for the day, imagine him or her telling you that you have a healthy set of teeth. If you have a meeting scheduled with your mortgage application, imagine it being accepted.

Think of how you will enter your workplace, welcomed by a smiling boss and group of co-workers. Replace things that happened in a negative manner with a more positive outcome. In your mind's eye, twist the negative occurrences into positive. Think that things went really well.

Just before you go to bed try to practice visualization. When we sleep our conscious mind is at rest, but our subconscious mind is super active. By practicing visualization just before we go to bed, we train our subconscious to be occupied by events as we want them to be. The subconscious mind does not distinguish between imagined reality and reality.

For our subconscious forces, everything that enters it is real. When the subconscious mind believes something to be real, it drives our actions in sync with these thoughts and leads to the manifestation of our imagined thoughts. This is how we bring about a change in our thought frequency from negative to positive via visualization. You are simply filling your mind with limitless positive energy, which gives you hope and fills the mind with positivity to give you plenty of possibilities.

Reframe Disappointment

Don't think of disappointment as a catastrophe after which your world comes crashing down. There is life beyond disappointment, so think of it as a normal occurrence. Don't be too hard on yourself. You can't possibly do everything exceptionally well. It is alright to have a few downs, too, along with the ups. Some folks find it increasingly challenging to move past their failures and get caught in a vicious web of negative thoughts and action. Allow yourself to experience disappointment and look at any situation in an objective manner.

Learn to segregate situations that are within and beyond your control. For instance, you performed a project to the best of your abilities and the client's brief. However, they changed their brief and want to make changes in the project before accepting it. It is natural to be disappointed and affected by this since you worked so hard on it. However, this isn't something that is a consequence of your action. Sometimes, you have to let go of matters that are not within your realm of control. Focus instead on things that can be controlled. For instance, better communication and brainstorming with the client during the initial stages of the project to help them understand exactly what they want. Think of different ways to improve client brief and communication, so clarity is established right at the onset of the project.

This will help you move towards a more constructive frame of mind and break away from the negative thinking pattern.

NLP and Context Reframing

The core of NLP is programming your mind by reframing thoughts using the main NLP presumption that every action or piece of behavior is valuable in a specific situation. By thinking of NLP in terms of every action or behavior being used in a specific situation, you change the response to that specific behavior. Consider multiple factors that can be reframed to obtain a drastically different response.

For instance, if you share a situation with a friend and think about things from their perspective, you will get a different spin on the same issue. Notice how a positive spin is given to ideas in a political scenario using NLP. When you believe every behavior has a more positive intention, the shift changes from negative to neutral thoughts. For instance, you think about hurting someone with your words or actions. There is still a positive intention behind it. It is to feel secure, powerful and completely in control. It can also be to prevent the other person from doing something wrong or to make them a better person through punishment.

Every situation is good in some way. Our brains process everything in evolutionary terms with an underlying purpose. A majority of the time, we work for the overall benefit or survival of everyone involved. However, there are times when we act with a short haul personal interest, but there is always a clear objective of our responses and actions. Identify the underlying positive in every situation, response or behavior.

Dissociation

A knee-jerk, or quick, reaction to any seemingly negative situation when one is frustrated or stressed is natural. Think about your reaction when your boss yells at you, you have an argument with your spouse or have to wait endlessly for a client who has made a habit of showing up late for every meeting. NLP helps mitigate the effects of these damaging feelings by restoring greater objectivity and neutrality in any situation.

Recognize the emotion that you want to eliminate. Imagine yourself living the entire situation from a third person point of view. Let this mental scenario unfold before you in rewind and then set it to fast forward. Add humorous background music to it to make the situation lighter. Play it in your mind a couple of times. Try to visualize the scene as it's playing currently. The negative feelings should evaporate or decrease. It can also be changed. The pattern can be repeated multiple times for higher impact.

Anchor Yourself

Anchor yourself to associate a specific positive emotion or response with a particular sensation. When you identify a positive emotion by linking it to a deliberate gesture, the anchor can be stimulated each time you are feeling low. You will gradually notice your feelings or emotions beginning to transform.

Recognize what you want to experience by recalling a time you were extremely happy or your life was full of joy. Make that visual sharp, powerful and intense. Remember that time by performing a physical action such as rubbing your palms or touching your nose. Repeat this until you find an anchoring phrase signifying happy times closely linked with the physical gesture. Once your mind is conditioned to associate the gesture with an anchor phrase, you will find yourself thinking about the happy time simply by performing the gesture.

 By performing the gesture, your mood will alter from frustration, stress and anger to a state of calmness, confidence and joy. This is an excellent strategy for altering your mood quickly.

Establish Rapport

There are plenty of ways to get along with people for rapport building. One of them is focusing on the other person's breathing. Another great way to establish rapport on a subconscious level is to mirror the person's body language, including gestures, posture, expressions and words. This works on a very subconscious and primordial level. The theory is deeply rooted in evolutionary science.

When you mirror someone's actions, at a subconscious level you are revealing to them that you are similar. However, this should be subtle. Don't give the other person an impression that you are imitating him or her, or else they could be offended.

When someone sits with their legs crossed, subtly follow their actions and cross your legs. When someone leans or rests their elbow on a bar table, you can follow suit. Similarly, when the other person takes a sip of the drink from his or her glass, follow it up by taking a sip from your glass, too.

I would go one step more and recommend trying to recognize which is their primary sensory perception (visual, kinesthetic, or auditory) and then model your communication pattern on the same. For instance, if you identify that a particular person is primarily visual, phrases such as, "I see you buddy," or, "I am seeing this," can work wonders. Similarly, if a person is fundamentally auditory in perception, "I hear what you are saying," or, "I am hearing this right," is a great way to build a rapport with other people.

Changing Beliefs

When you use the content reframing technique, the number of beliefs that limit you are restricted. However, reframing can be challenging when it comes to a previously held belief. Changing a previously held belief requires a different approach altogether. For instance, if you've had a difficult relationship in the past, you are likely to believe that every partner you'll have will only make life challenging for you.

To alter a limiting belief, gather all positive evidence in support of the situation or circumstances. Think of as much good as you can. For instance, think about all the wonderful relationships around you that reinforce the fact that happy, fulfilling relationships are very much a possibility. Think about the meaningful and fulfilling relationship shared by your parents or friends. Look around for the good to challenge your negative beliefs. Think about partners who have been loving and respectful towards you.

Keep affirming the opposite of your self-limiting belief by saying something like, "I will find a wonderful partner who will understand, support and inspire me." Keep repeating this thought until it is completely absorbed by the unconscious mind. After about a month of repetition, you will begin to notice a difference in beliefs.

Chapter Six: Using the Empty Chair Technique

'Gestalt' refers to the idea that the whole is often greater than the total of its parts. It was founded by Fritz Perls and relies on the idea that an entire or complete being is linked to their environment, memories, thoughts and loved ones. Therefore, gestalt techniques are utilized for helping therapists to engage client's inner feelings, thoughts, emotions (to bring about awareness of the present) and actions by a series of interactive techniques, one of which is the empty chair technique.

The 'empty chair' is another widely used gestalt therapy technique for bringing about a shift in thoughts through conversation with an imaginary person. The person undertakes a role-play talk with an imagined friend, family member or another specific individual sitting across from them on the empty chair (hence, 'empty chair' technique). The aim of the empty chair technique is to talk about things that you wouldn't discuss with them in person.

For instance, you are jealous of your friend being more successful, richer and happier than you, which is the reason why you're developing feelings of hatred towards them. You know the feelings of hatred are not triggered by their acts but your own perception of their life in comparison to yours. You can't vocalize these feelings to your friend, or you might risk losing them.

Therefore, you aim to achieve a sort of emotional catharsis by pouring your heart out to the friend in an imaginary manner. Sometimes, it is also done to rehearse something that you want to say to a person but haven't been able to muster the courage yet. Another person (your therapist or a close friend) can play as the other person sitting on the opposite chair.

When Is It Used?

The empty chair technique is primarily used for integrating different components or disjoined parts of an individual's personality or life to derive a greater psychotherapeutic insight of the prevailing challenges. It helps move people from a place of simply talking about an issue to immediate fullness and present experience or sensation of it, thus affecting their action and cognition as a result.

The less likely you are to verbalize your thoughts and feelings, the likelier it is that therapists will use this technique to get you to vocalize and experience the sensation of verbalizing your thoughts. It is ideally not used for people who are already experiencing or expressing a surge of emotions.

How Does It Help?

The empty chair technique draws the client into the present for immediate experiences. Verbalizations often transform into enlivened moments. At times, we are not able to feel or sense the series of conflicts going on in our mind. Though there are overpowering feelings, we don't experience living these feelings until we vocalize them. Once you live through or get a sense of your thoughts as they unfold in person, you realize what it is.

Any type of intervention (including the empty chair technique) which fights the client's passivity and turns psychotherapy into a fulfilling collaboration works well. Sometimes, simply talking or vocalizing our feelings gives us a totally different perspective on the issue that we hadn't initially considered.

How Exactly Does One Practice the Empty Chair?

You sit facing an empty chair and visualizes the individual that you see as the cause of the challenging situation or conflict. You can also imagine 'it' to be a part of your personality. You start talking to the empty chair, explicitly expressing your thoughts, emotions, feelings and perspective of the situation.

There is another angle to it which is rather interesting. Once you completely verbalize your thoughts, you switch places and sit on the empty chair. Then, placing yourself in the shoes of the other person, you respond to yourself as you think they might.. You simply assume their role and speak things from his or her perspective.

For instance, in the above example, if you find yourself hating your close friends out of a feeling of jealousy, you get talking about it. Then, when you place yourself on the other person's chair (or shoes), in the flow of vocalizing their thoughts, you can realize many things you may not have considered earlier such as how hard your friend works or the stress he or she goes through to maintain their lifestyle or live the life you envy.

There may be a huge amount of stress, exhaustion and competitiveness they have to deal with on a daily basis. On the exterior, your life may not be as exciting or glamour packed as theirs, but you enjoy your work and are passionate about it. You work at your own pace and enjoy it. You have more time for other pursuits and passions, along with the privilege of spending more time with loved ones.

When you start vocalizing your thoughts, the subconscious often lets your speech flow through thoughts in an unrestrained manner to help you view things from a different perspective. You will begin to look at things from a different angle that you hadn't considered before while thinking things only from your point of view. A person can switch chairs back and forth as required to have a meaningful dialogue. This will allow the situation to unfold with several answers and insights.

If the opposite chair symbolizes a part of you or a challenging internal conflict, you will explore different aspects of the self and gain an insight of your own struggles. This self-discovery or discovery of the other person's perspective is the essence of empty chair therapy.

Chapter Seven: Proven Tips for Managing Internal Dialogues

I know you've heard this a million times by now, but I never tire of saying or hearing it because it is 100 percent true, "We create our own reality." There are no two ways about it. You create your own reality with how you perceive it. This is often reinforced by the human mind potential crowd, who believes that our thoughts often become our destiny. Reality is nothing but attention or interpretation of an act. The way you interpret a certain act becomes your reality.

For instance, if your manager is under tremendous pressure, and he or she screams at you one fine day without any apparent reason, your perception that he or she doesn't like you becomes your reality. The reality, in this case, is nothing but your perception, which may or may not be true. This perception is more often than not derived through internal dialogues.

The internal dialogue is actually our ego conversing with itself. It is the voice that combines reasons and feelings with people, situations and life events. Internal dialogue is often the filter through which we extract meaning from our everyday life. When your internal dialogue is full of negativity, frustration and gloominess, your reality or perception becomes equally gloomy. Similarly, when your internal filter is filled with positivity, optimism and uplifting internal dialogue, that becomes the frame of your life, and consequently, your reality.

Thus, think of your internal dialogue as a blank canvas that can be painted with just about anything that you want to. Want to manage your internal dialogue more effectively? Here are some proven tips to help you deal with your internal dialogue in a more rewarding and fulfilling manner:

Develop the Art of Gratitude

Gratitude is a potent mental state that leads to a complete transformation of our internal framework. It shifts the focus for what we need or don't have in our lives to our blessings, which places us in a more positive frame of mind. All you need to do is affirm all the things you are grateful for by saying something like, "I am truly grateful for ...." Recount all the things you are thankful for, including things you take for granted such as your eyesight, the limbs you walk on, the clothes you wear and the roof above your head.

By counting your blessings, you are creating a positive momentum for a powerful internal dialogue. What you are doing is training your subconscious mind to be more alert towards attracting more of these blessings. You are invariably drawing more gratitude worthy instances and experiences in your life. Remember, your energy follows your attention. Whatever you give attention to for long is where your energy goes. This can bring about a huge shift in your internal dialogue.

Sidestep Negativity

There's little doubt about the fact that negativity is all around us. Our brain is wired to pick up negativity faster than positivity in any situation. This has been a direct result of evolution, where our ancestors were neurologically conditioned to look for dangers or risks around them as the result of a deep-rooted survival mentality. Everything that our ancestors did would revolve around their fears related to food, shelter and safety. This is exactly why we are wired to sense the threat and negativity around us faster than the positives.

Instead of enjoying the present meal, we think about our next meal. Instead of enjoying the present, we are bogged down with concerns of the past. It is deeply rooted in our nervous system and prevents us from seeing the positivity around us. Consciously commit to avoiding the negative and focusing only on the positive.

Negativity pollutes our internal self-talk with destructive emotions such as fear, jealousy, anger, frustration and other similar emotions. While the entire negativity cannot be avoided overnight, we can purposefully try refocusing our attention from the negative to the positive, which can have a powerful impact on our overall internal dialogue.

Spend Time Being Still

Meditation is one of the best ways of conquering your internal dialogue. You'll be shocked to know that our mind is occupied by at least 70,000 to 80,000 individual thoughts per day. When you calm or silence the hyperactive mind, you create a blank canvas for starting with a positive and constructive internal dialogue. Think of your post-meditation mind as a highly fertile ground, where you can plant just about any seeds for cultivating positive and receptive thoughts and dialogues.

Meditation increases our awareness and helps us develop greater mindfulness towards the mind's contents to bring about a more constructive internal dialogue. Only when we bring about a sense of mental clarity can we condition the mind to override negative feelings or train the mind to think positive thoughts through repetition.

Channelize Affirmations

Affirmations are powerful, positive ways to reframe the subconscious mind. Think about your mind as a software application that can be easily reprogrammed from negative to positive with the help of a few codes. These codes are nothing but affirmations or positive statements that allow us to replace negative thoughts with more positive or constructive thoughts.

They replace old and obsolete thoughts with fresher and more inspiring thoughts that allow the subconscious to drive our action in the same direction. We are led to live those thoughts through our actions guided by the subconscious mind.

When you keep practicing and repeating these affirmations, they change your internal dialogue and belief.

Your attention is focused on what you desire rather than what you don't.

Practice Perfect Speech and Behavior

Our speech, actions and behavior are a direct result of our internal dialogue. They support or are an extension of the conversations that take place within us. Our actions are a result of our thoughts, but it also works the other way around. The actions also impact our thoughts and internal dialogue. When you are more mindful of your speech and action, you pave the way for a refined, meaningful and positive internal dialogue. Being conscious allows you to focus on behavior that invariably results in positive afterthoughts.

Remember Who You Are

Never forget your essential nature while being swept by material considerations, ego, societal hype and other components. We tend to lose our true spirit in the clutter and noise going on around us. The true objective or spirit of our nature is totally lost when we disconnect with our pure consciousness.

When we remember who will essentially are, our internal dialogue shifts from being negative to being a reflection of complete awareness. Complete awareness of the self helps to keep the internal dialogue positive, inspiring and uplifting.

Give Your Inner Critic a Name

Separate your inner critic from you by giving it a distinct name and persona. It isn't a part of who or what you are. It is simply a perspective from another person's point of view. It isn't who you are or what you think about yourself. This will help you look at the critical side in a more objective manner and not as something that defines you. You will take it.

When you create a psychological entity by speaking or giving the inner critic a second or third person, you reduce negative feelings of stress and anxiety. It gives you the power to manage and regulate emotions while reducing discomfort.

Also, allow the conversation to flow around your goals. Don't feed negative self-talk by indulging in conversations that deviate from your primary goals.

Chapter Eight: Dealing with Internal Conflicts

During many situations in life, we are torn between logic and emotions. Our rational mind and emotions are not in sync. How do you deal with conflicts arising as a result of disagreement or conflict between heart and mind or even conflict between two overpowering emotions? Here are a few tried and tested tips that can help you deal with internal conflicts to increase your emotional intelligence:

Identify that There Is Internal Conflict

The first step towards dealing with internal conflict is to identify that there is a situation of internal conflict. Identify that there is a conflict that you are struggling with. Acknowledge that a situation of conflict has come up and that it has to be dealt with in a manner where the conflict is effectively resolved.

For instance, suppose your family wants you to work in its business since there is no heir to look after it or take it ahead. You, on the other hand, want to become a painter and are not interested or have the acumen for business. This is a clear conflict of the heart versus mind.

Sometimes, there can be a huge conflict of emotions, too. You may have to choose between your friend and a partner (who is probably an ex-partner of the friend). These situations arise when we have to choose between two people or two emotions.

You may want to do something like volunteer for a cause, but all your time is spent earning money for survival, and hence, there is a conflict between emotions and practical considerations.

One of the worst ways to resolve an internal conflict is trying to pretend that there is no conflict. Don't deny the existence of a conflict. Rather, accept it and find ways to deal with it.

Experience the Conflict

Every time you experience a clash between emotions, consider the situation for a moment and notice your feelings. Be mindful of the physical sensations experienced while feeling the emotion. Do your legs shake while feeling the emotion? Do you suddenly start feeling warm? Does your throat go dry while experiencing these emotions?

Once you identify the physiological feelings, it is easy to associate it with an emotion or conflict. For instance, you know your face becomes hot and red when you get angry. This helps you connect the physiological function of hotness and redness of the face with anger. This technique of processing your emotions is referred to as 'sensing.' Once you have identified the emotion, give it a name. For example, you decide to call it rage.

Next, you think about how the emotion is interfering with your daily life. You may be fuming because of something a trusted friend said behind your back. At the same time, your heart is just not ready to accept that he or she could betray you in such a manner. How do you feel about this emotion? Is it interfering with your ability to think about other constructive things? Is there any way to act on the overpowering feelings or emotions? Is there a healthy outlet to give vent to the conflict?

Choose a healthy way to release this conflict until you find a solution. You may want to go on a long walk alone, pour your heart to someone about it, engage in your favorite hobby, travel, paint or play a musical instrument. This will give you a good grip on your conflict for the moment and make it subside until you have a clear solution.

Avoid Feeling Guilty About Your Emotions

While thoughts are rational, we often tend to view emotions as irrational, intense or something that can't be relied on. While we often think our thoughts are right, your emotions aren't always wrong or irrational. If anything, they are reliable indicators of how you think and feel about people and situations. Don't feel guilty about emotions that do not match your logical thoughts.

For instance, logically, your manager is amazing at his or her work and you admire him or her for their accomplishments. However, you also experience pangs of envy each time you are around them. There is a conflict between your rational thought that admires them and the emotion that envies them. Don't feel guilty about your emotions not being in sync with your thoughts. Think of them objectively as emotions. Let them live their life and pass. Feeling ashamed of emotions that are not in line with your thoughts only increases conflict.

Avoid Second Guessing Once You Make Up Your Mind

Once you've made up your mind, there is no need to ruminate over every decision. Second guessing only increases the intensity of the conflict. You'll find yourself doubting the way you chose multiple times. To eliminate all the confusion, have complete faith in your decisions and go with what you've decided.

Have confidence in your decisions when you make them rather than second guessing each decision. When you live your decisions without thinking about them multiple times, you experience less emotional conflict.

Stick to Your Values Rather than Being Influenced by Others

Rather than being influenced by others or having too many voices clouding your opinion, stick to your own core values while making important decisions. Listening too much to people can create a conflict of emotions, beliefs and thoughts. People will offer you advice or suggestions from their perspective, which may not be in agreement with your core beliefs and values.

Stop fussing about what other people think and do what is in sync with your thoughts, values and beliefs to better manage or avoid conflict. Don't be easily influenced by others and ask yourself questions such as what you think of the situation. How will your decision impact yourself and others? Who will face the consequences of your decision? Does this decision reflect your values, or are you towing someone else's value system? Think about what you value and what is important for you as a person. This will eliminate any conflict from arising.

Write Down the Conflict

One of the best ways to deal with conflict is to write it down in explicit terms. This way, you unload the unwanted conflict from the brain and dump it on paper, which can provide you with great relief. The act of writing can give you complete self-understanding by viewing things from a different perspective, which helps in conflict resolution.

Chapter Nine: Dealing with Your Past

If you are still living in painful memories or carry any emotional baggage from the past, you are not paving the way for an emotionally healthy and balanced future. You'll have a hard time creating a happy and positive life ahead of you if you are still wrestling with the past. When you accept the past rather than obsessing about it, and deal with it, you are creating avenues for a more rewarding life.

Here are a few brilliant tips for dealing with the past and living a more positive, balanced and emotionally fulfilling life:

Acknowledge Past Challenges

Unresolved experiences of the past can create not only lasting physical damage but psychological consequences as well. Don't let these destructive emotions of shame, guilt, regret, revenge, etc. breed inside you for long. Learn to come to terms with these emotions so as to not let your present or future be affected by them.

Don't pretend that you are not affected by these events. You won't be in a position to get over it if you pretend that it didn't happen. Try to acknowledge and allow yourself to feel everything that you felt in the past (and still feel).

For instance, if you feel an overpowering emotion triggered by memories of the past, instead of curbing the feeling, step away for some time. Use this time to reflect on your emotions and how they impact you. Once you are done reflecting upon and feeling the emotions, get back to what you were doing. The consequence of past actions can be very powerful, especially if you are without a support system.

At times, the trauma from past actions is so overpowering that it impacts our relationships. Past trauma can also prevent you from fulfilling your goals. This affects not just your present perspective about life but also your ability to deal with challenges in life.

Understand that There's No Way to Change the Past

There is nothing you can do to change the past. As much as you wish to, you can't do anything to change events or people. The best way to manage a painful past is to tell yourself that it can't be changed now, accept it and change the way you perceive it.

There are many things that are outside our circle of control. However, the way we react to them is something that is still in our hands. We can either live in the past and ruin our present and future, or we can choose to learn from the past and move on. Even though plenty of circumstances are beyond our control, accepting these events as being a part of life is something that is completely within our realm of control.

The past cannot be revisited, but perception about it can be changed. If you don't stop obsessing over the past, the hurt will spill over and damage future experiences.

Direct your efforts towards accepting the past and offering forgiveness to the ones who have hurt you. You don't do this for them; you do it for your own peace and well-being. You give forgiveness to let go of the past and move on. Feel the emotions you want to feel and then let go after a point.

Try to remind yourself that hanging on to these destructive emotions will only end up harming you. Acknowledge the negative emotions and seek compassion for others as well as yourself. Gather all the strength to forgive everyone who harmed you.

Don't expect this to be an overnight process. It will differ from person to person and may take time.

Spend Time with Different People

Spending time in the same setting with the same people where you experienced negative past emotions will only trigger more of the same reactions. Instead, change your setting or spend time with a different group of people who are supportive, inspiring and positive. A powerful social support system can safeguard you from damaging experiences.

Support other people around you who are feeling low to derive strength from their situation and support them. Volunteering is one of the most wonderful ways to let go of a painful past and build a positive and constructive present which will serve as a foundation for a good future. It will also be a great way to interact with a new set of people. When you see other people's vulnerabilities, you become more thankful for your blessings and learn to cope with your troubles.

Seek the Help of a Professional

If you are feeling overwhelmed by your past and nothing else seems to work, seek the help of a professional counselor or therapist. There are instances when experiences can be devastating and can threaten to change your entire life ahead. In such cases, professional intervention is required. Talk to therapists who will help you with a series of therapies to move on from the past.

If nothing else, simply talking to a professional will help you see things from a more objective perspective.

Examine Your Social Circle

Consider moving away from friends who compel you to live in the past. Your immediate social environment will play an essential role when it comes to helping you let go of the past. It also defines who you are and affects your experiences. An encouraging, positive and supportive social circle that doesn't make you stay in the past can change the way you look at things.

I would recommend spending time with people who make you laugh or help you feel good about yourself. Stay away from folks who encourage negative habits or make you feel miserable about yourself. These are the type of people who will only stop your emotional growth or development. For instance, friends who constantly try to put you down or keep reminding you of the past may not be good news. Try making new friends in a different setting. This is will get you out of your comfort zone and facilitate personal growth.

Try new hobbies with new friends. Join a hobby group on social media or a local hobby club where you can interact with people who share similar interests. Fresh directions in life can open avenues you hadn't thought were possible earlier.

Systematic Desensitization

Systematic desensitization is a technique through which you are gradually relieving yourself of a potentially destructive situation with a series of relaxation techniques. The objective is to be at ease while exploring different stress relief methods.

Start with simple relaxation techniques such as deep breathing, exercising and meditation. Each time you find yourself exposed to a situation that stresses you as it reminds you of a past experience, you can practice these relaxation techniques to stay calm. The idea is to progress at your pace without rushing yourself to eliminate the pain. You should be able to engage confidently in situations that cause you distress over a period of time

For instance, if you had a terrible experience while addressing an audience on the stage earlier, you may avoid all opportunities to speak on stage. A past experience comes to haunt you each time you think of going on the stage. Get past this by actively opting to address an audience. Start with a small group of friends or co-workers in a meeting room or your home.

Employ relaxation techniques each time you find yourself being a bundle of nerves before speaking. Gradually, go with a bigger audience. There will come a time when you will be completely confident about addressing an audience without any fear. Keep going slowly, steadily and consistently. It may not be easy in the beginning, but eventually, you'll gather the confidence to master the art of speaking to an audience without being nervous.

Chapter Ten: The Art of Forgiving People

Forgiving people is important for emotional and spiritual growth. Your negative experience of how someone has hurt you is nothing but a negative energy you carry in your mind. These feelings of anger, revenge, hatred, rage and more gradually take away your power to focus on constructive and positive things by occupying space in your mind. When you release it, you should award or gift yourself more peace. Here are some tips for practicing forgiveness and letting your mind be occupied by more positive emotions:

Don't Sleep Angry

Before going to bed, don't spend valuable time reviewing anything negative that you don't want to be reinforced in your subconscious because as we discussed earlier, the subconscious is the most active when we are asleep. Focus on positive and constructive thoughts just before going to bed rather than harboring hatred. If you have had an argument or disagreement with someone, talk to them and clear the air before going to bed. Focus on ending it on a positive note even if you don't wish to associate with the person in future.

Be grateful and peaceful in aligning with your values and who you are as a person. Associate with people who possess the same beliefs and ideals as you. You are in control of how your mind is programmed just before going to sleep, which means you should only focus on positive thoughts.

Learn to Let Go like Water

Don't be forceful or try to one-up people in pointless ego battles. Rather be like water that just flows. Be soft, accommodating, tolerant and flexible of other opinions rather than forcing your views on others. Instead of focusing on telling and talking, concentrate on listening. When someone says something that is contrary to your argument, say something like, "I've never thought about it like this before, thank you for introducing me to a new point of view. I'll sure think about it."

Focus on Being Kind Instead of Being Right

When your mind is consumed by revenge, you are actually digging a grave for yourself, too. Resentment is destructive for you. The world isn't always hunky dory. People behave the way they do because that's just how they are. That's how they believe they are supposed to behave, and there's nothing much you can do about it unless it's a legally punishable offense. However, processing your reaction is something you can choose.

Get rid of the need to prove others wrong or to reinforce the idea that something bad has happened to you.

Think of a scenario where someone hurts you by saying something offensive. Rather than harboring feelings of resentment, you just disconnect or remove yourself from the situation and choose to react with kindness. You choose to send energies of joy and forgiveness rather than reacting in a negative manner. This is something you can do to maintain your internal balance and harmony. Focus on being compassionate more than being right.

Don't Actively Seek Occasions to be Offended

Don't keep looking for opportunities to be offended. Many people spend a huge amount of energy looking for occasions to be hurt. It can be a discourteous stranger, a person swearing around you, someone disagreeing with your views on social media or just about anything that ticks you off. Become a person who isn't offended by the tiniest of things or a series of circumstances.

Think About How No One is Perfect

Think about the person who has hurt you. He or she is a human with his or her own strengths and shortcomings. They are acting from their own limited beliefs and personality traits, for which you don't have to punish yourself. Their frame of reference may not be the same as yours.

While you were feeling hurt, the other person is trying to meet their own needs. What was the need of the other individual? Why do you think they behaved in a hurtful manner towards you? This will help you consider things from their perspective or be empathetic towards their situation despite being hurt.

Chapter Eleven: Perceptual Positions

Perceptual Positions in NLP refers to considering a situation from the first, second and third-person perspective.

The first position is your regular, daily experience about any event or experience. In the first-person perspective, or first perceptual position, you are completely connected with the experience through subjective filters. It is a personal, subjective experience that is free from another person's perspective.

The second-person perspective, or second perceptual position, is when you assume things from another person's point of view. Typically, salespeople, negotiators and counselors are remarkably good at the second perceptual position. They are processing information from the other person's perceptual experiences. This is done to empathize with the other person or understand their mind map.

The third-person perspective, or third perceptual position, is when you assume the role of an objective observer and consider perceptual experiences from an objective point of view or that of an external observer, much like watching a movie.

How Do You Assume a Second Position?

The second position is the position of modeling, learning and absorbing. It is like activating neurons in your nervous system that are dormant within the observer but boast of the same neuron functions as the neurons in the person you are modeling after.

The next time you find yourself in the company of a person you want to emulate, try these helpful tips:

- Clear your mind completely.

- Try to match your breathing rhythm or pattern with the person you want to emulate or empathize with.

- Practice micro muscle mirroring. For example, if the other individual moves their legs, move your leg muscles slightly as if you are about to move your legs. Feel your leg muscles moving before lifting them. Practice this with full body movements.

The objective of the practice is to experience the world as if you are the other person. Imagine yourself assuming their body, so you become them.

How do You Assume a Third Person Position?

Perform an activity, and during the activity move to a position that offers you a clear unobstructed view of the space where you just performed the activity. Take on a straight, upright position with shoulders pulled back. Imagine watching yourself in the performance space. Doing it this way, you can give unbiased feedback. It is like watching a movie or theatre performance.

Conclusion

Thank you for getting a copy of *Emotional Intelligence: The Essential Guide to Improving Your Social Skills, Relationships and Boosting Your EQ.*

I genuinely hope you enjoyed reading this book and that you were able to master proven strategies for increasing your emotional and social intelligence.

I've included lots of practical pointers, actionable techniques and wisdom nuggets to help boost your emotional intelligence and enjoy rewarding relationships.

One of the best parts of emotional intelligence is that it can be constantly increased, unlike intelligence quotient (which is more or less pre-determined).

The next step is to implement all the proven techniques mentioned in this book. Reading this book is not going to increase your emotional quotient unless you apply these techniques in your daily life. Of course, you won't miraculously transform into an emotionally intelligent being in a day or two. However, you'll gradually get there by consistently following these techniques over a period of time.

Finally, if you found this book useful in any way, a review on Amazon is always appreciated!

28405195R00053

Made in the USA
Middletown, DE
20 December 2018